I0424320

This Journal Belongs To: